INTRODUCTION

The ability to sight-read fluently is a most important part of your training as a violinist, whether you intend to play professionally, or simply for enjoyment. Yet the *study* of sight-reading is often badly neglected by young players and is frequently regarded as no more than a rather unpleasant side-line. If you become a *good* sight-reader you will be able to learn pieces more quickly, and play in ensembles and orchestras with confidence and assurance. Also, in grade examinations, good performance in the sight-reading test will result in useful extra marks!

Using the workbook

The purpose of this workbook is to incorporate sight-reading regularly into your practice and lessons, and to help you prepare for the sight-reading test in grade examinations. It offers you a progressive series of enjoyable and stimulating stages in which, with careful work, you should show considerable improvement from week to week.

Each stage consists of two parts: firstly, exercises which you should prepare in advance, along with a short piece with questions; and secondly, an unprepared test, to be found at the end of the book.

Your teacher will mark your work according to accuracy. Each stage carries a maximum of 50 marks and your work will be assessed as follows:

> 2 marks for each of the six questions relating to the prepared piece (total 12)
> 18 marks for the prepared piece itself.
> 20 marks for the unprepared test. (Teachers should devise a similar series of questions for the unprepared test, and take the answers into account when allocating a final mark.)

Space is given at the end of each stage for you to keep a running total of your marks as you progress. If you are scoring 40 or more each time you are doing well!

At the top of the first page in each stage you will see one or two new features to be introduced. There are then four different types of exercise:

1 **Rhythmic exercises** It is very important that you should be able to feel and maintain a steady beat. These exercises will help develop this ability. There are at least four ways of doing these exercises: clap or tap the lower line (the beat) while singing the upper line to 'la'; tap the lower line with your foot and clap the upper line; on a table or flat surface, tap the lower line with one hand and the upper line with the other; 'play' the lower line on a metronome and clap or tap the upper line.

2 **Melodic exercises** Fluent sight-reading depends on recognising melodic shapes at first glance. These shapes are often related to scales and arpeggios. Before you begin, always notice the *key-signature* and the notes affected by it, then work out the finger patterns on the finger board.

3 **A prepared piece with questions** You should prepare carefully both the piece and the questions, which are to help you think about and understand the piece before you play it. Put your answers in the spaces provided.

4 **An unprepared piece** Finally, your teacher will give you an *unprepared* test to be read at *sight*. Make sure you have read the *Sight-reading Checklist* on page 17 before you begin each piece.

Remember to count throughout each piece and to keep going at a steady and even tempo. Always try to look ahead, at least to the next note or beat.

NAME

EXAMINATION RECORD

Grade	Date	Mark

TEACHER'S NAME

TELEPHONE

© 1993 by Faber Music Ltd
First published in 1993 by Faber Music Ltd
3 Queen Square London WC1N 3AU
Music and text set by Silverfen
Cover illustration by Drew Hillier
Printed in England by Caligraving Ltd
All rights reserved

ISBN 0-571-51387-5

STAGE 1

E minor

$\frac{5}{4}$

RHYTHMIC EXERCISES

MELODIC EXERCISES

PREPARED PIECE

Marks*

1 In which key is this piece written?

2 What does *Allegretto ritmico* mean?

3 What is the character of this piece?

4 Mark the first note affected by the key-signature.

5 How will you count this piece?

6 What does *poco dim.* (bar 15) mean?

Total:

Allegretto ritmico

Unprepared tests page 18

Mark:

Prepared work total:

Unprepared:

Total:

*The mark boxes are to be filled in by your teacher (see Introduction).

STAGE 2

3ʳᵈ Position

RHYTHMIC EXERCISES

MELODIC EXERCISES

PREPARED PIECE

1 What does *Allegro moderato* mean? ☐

2 How will you give character to your performance? ☐

3 What does the figure 1 over the D in bar two indicate? ☐

4 How many times does the rhythm of bar 1 return? ☐

5 What will you count? ☐

6 In which key is this piece? ☐

Total: ☐

Unprepared tests page 19

Mark: ☐

Prepared work total: ☐

Unprepared: ☐

Total: ☐

Running totals:

1	2

STAGE 3

RHYTHMIC EXERCISES

1

2

3

MELODIC EXERCISES

1

2

3

4

PREPARED PIECE

1 In which key is this piece written?

2 What does *Lento espressivo* mean?

3 How will that marking affect your performance?

4 Where does the music of the opening two bars return?

5 In what ways do the two versions differ?

6 How will you count this piece?

Total:

Unprepared tests page 20

Mark:

Prepared work total:

Unprepared:

Total:

Running totals:

1	2	3

STAGE 4

More patterns in 3/8

RHYTHMIC EXERCISES

MELODIC EXERCISES

PREPARED PIECE

1 In which key is this piece written?

2 What does *Andantino* mean?

3 What is the character of this piece?

4 How will you count this piece?

5 What is the duration of the first note?

6 What does the sign ⌢ over the last note indicate?

Total:

Unprepared tests page 21

Mark:

Prepared work total:

Unprepared:

Total:

Running totals:

1	2	3	4

STAGE 5

E major
3
2

RHYTHMIC EXERCISES

1

2

3

MELODIC EXERCISES

1

2

3

PREPARED PIECE

1 What does *Moderato, tempo di valse* mean?

2 How will you give character to your performance?

3 How many times does the rhythm of bar 1 return?

4 Clap the rhythm:

5 Where does it occur?

6 In which key is this piece written? Mark a cross above the first D♯.

Total:

Moderato, tempo di valse

mf ——————————————— *p*

6

cresc.

11

rit.

4

Unprepared tests page 22

Mark:

Prepared work total:

Unprepared:

Total:

Running totals:

1	2	3	4	5

STAGE 6

E♭ major

RHYTHMIC EXERCISES

1

2

3

MELODIC EXERCISES

1

2

3

4

PREPARED PIECE

1 How many beats are there in each bar?

2 In which key is the piece written?

3 What does *mf* indicate?

4 What does the marking 𝄾 𝄾 indicate?

5 What is the meaning of *Moderato, tempo di minuetto*?

6 Clap this rhythm:

Total:

Moderato, tempo di minuetto

Unprepared tests page 23

Mark:

Prepared work total:

Unprepared:

Total:

Running totals:

1	2	3	4	5	6

STAGE 7

More dotted rhythms
5
8

RHYTHMIC EXERCISES

MELODIC EXERCISES

PREPARED PIECE

1 In which key is this piece written?

2 What does *Grazioso* mean?

3 How will that marking affect your performance?

4 How will you count this piece?

5 How often does the rhythm of the opening bar return?

6 What does the marking 𝅘𝅥 𝅘𝅥 𝅘𝅥 𝅘𝅥 𝅘𝅥 (bars 9-11) indicate?

Total: ☐

Unprepared tests page 24

Mark: ☐

Prepared work total: ☐

Unprepared: ☐

Total: ☐

Running totals:

1	2	3	4	5	6	7

CONCLUSION

A sight-reading checklist

Before you begin to play a piece at sight, always remember to consider the following:

1 Look at the key-signature.

2 Look at the time-signature, and decide how you will count the piece.

3 Notice any accidentals that may occur.

4. Notice scale and arpeggio patterns.

5 Notice dynamic and other markings.

6 Look at the tempo mark and decide what speed to play. If the piece contains any fast passages, ensure you choose a speed you can maintain throughout.

7 Count one bar before you begin, to establish the speed.

When performing your sight-reading piece, always remember to:

1 CONTINUE TO COUNT THROUGHOUT THE PIECE.

2 Keep going at a steady and even tempo.

3 Ignore mistakes.

4 Check the key-signature at the beginning of each new line.

5 Look ahead – at least to the next beat or note.

6 Play *musically*.

UNPREPARED TESTS
STAGE 1

1   Con moto

6

11

2   Larghetto

4

8

3   Adagio ma non troppo

5

9

STAGE 2

STAGE 3

STAGE 4

1 Allegretto grazioso

mp cantabile

cresc.　　*f*　　*mp*

cresc.　　*f*　　*dim.*

2 Allegro vigoroso

f

mf　　*cresc.*　　*f*

p　　*cresc.*　　*f*

3 Siciliano

mp espressivo

mf

più lento　　rall.

STAGE 5

STAGE 6

STAGE 7